My Gulf world and me

Activity Book

Level 1

Activity Book

Level 1

by **Helen M Thomson** *and* **Salima Keshavjee**

T0385815

LWAYS LEARNING

PEARSON

Published by Pearson Education Limited,
Edinburgh Gate, Harlow, Essex, CM20 2JE.

Text © Pearson Education 2013

Edited by Kim Vernon
Designed by Juice Creative
Original illustrations © Pearson Education 2013
Illustrated by John Batten (Beehive illustration),
Gareth Clarke and Juice
Cover design by Juice
Cover photo © Shutterstock.com
Cover illustration by Gareth Clarke

First published 2013

20 19
IMP 10 9 8 7 6 5 4

British Library Cataloguing in Publication Data
A catalogue record for this book is available from
the British Library.

ISBN 978 0 435 15193 5

Printed in the UK by Ashford Colour Press Ltd

Acknowledgements
The author and publisher would like to thank
the following individuals and organisations for
permission to reproduce photographs:
(Key: b-bottom; c-centre; l-left; r-right; t-top)

Fotolia.com: 2 (football), 2 (honey cells), 2 (pattern),
7tl, 7cl, 8 (Ahmed), 8 (Ali), 8 (bike), 8 (Fatma),
8 (red car), 8 (Salim), 8 (Shamsa), 8 (Sharifa), 9 (cake),
9 (crab), 9 (ice cream), 9 (red car), 9-10 (starfish),
10 (bike), 10 (football), 10 (shell), 10 (tree), 16tl, 16cr,
17tl, 17tr, 17cl, 17bl, 17br, 19 (singing), 19 (swimming);
iStockphoto: 15c, 23c;
Kate Riddle © www.kateriddlephotography.com: 7tc,
7tr, 7c, 7cr, 8 (boat), 8 (boy running), 8 (school bus),
8 (taxi), 16tr, 16cl, 16bl, 16br, 17cr, 19 (apple), 19 (boy on
slide), 19 (jumping), 19 (running), 21tl, 21tr, 21cl, 21cr,
21bl, 21br, 22tl, 22tc, 22tr, 22bl, 22bc, 22br

All other images © Pearson Education

Contents

Shapes all around us

How many different shapes can you find in this picture?

Colour the shapes you find.

Fill in these sentences. Use the numbers in the box.

I can see _____ circles.

I can see _____ diamonds.

I can see _____ squares.

I can see _____ crescent.

I can see _____ triangles.

I can see _____ stars.

I can see _____ rectangles.

| one | two | three | four | five | six | seven | eight | nine | ten |

I

Shapes all around us

Count the number of sides.
The first one is done for you.

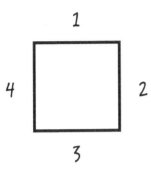

A square has _four_ sides.

A diamond has ____ sides.

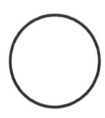

A circle has ____ side.

A crescent has ____ sides.

Did you know that a shape with six sides is called a hexagon? Here are some hexagons.

A triangle has ____ sides.

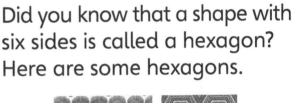

Can you draw a hexagon here?

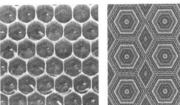

A rectangle has ____ sides.

2

Shapes all around us

Here are some rugs. What shapes can you see inside them? Write the names of the shapes under the rugs.

The first one is done for you.

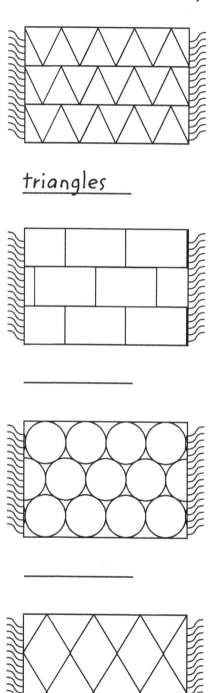

triangles

_____

_____

_____

Colour the rugs in.
Design your own rug here.

_____

3

Shapes all around us

Colour these shapes in lots of different colours.
Choose from these colours:

red

green

blue

black

yellow

Now you can play shape bingo. Good luck!

Shapes all around us

The names of the shapes are jumbled up. Put the letters in the correct order. Write the name beside the shape. The first one is done for you.

mdadion   *diamond* _____

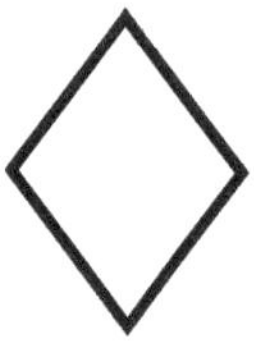

atrs   _____

rgetnclae   _____

seuqra   _____

crilec   _____

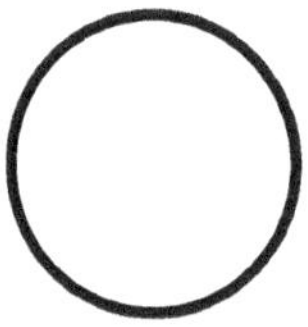

rtanigle   _____

cntrsece   _____

Getting from here to there

How many cars, buses, taxis, bikes and planes can you see?

Colour the cars blue, the buses yellow, the taxis red, the bikes green and the planes black.

I can see _____ cars.

I can see _____ buses.

I can see _____ taxis.

I can see _____ bikes.

I can see _____ planes.

Can you see any abras? Where are they?

_____

6

Getting from here to there

Listen and write the first letter of each word.

ACTIVITY

2

____lane

____us

____axi

____ike

____bra

____alk

Find the words in
this grid. Circle them.
One is done for you.

w	e	r	t	p	s	a	w	e
a	s	d	e	v	g	m	u	l
a	e	r	o	p	l	a	n	e
m	b	v	c	x	g	f	d	s
r	v	b	i	k	e	h	j	l
z	x	c	v	b	n	m	l	k
w	a	l	k	e	a	b	r	a
a	e	b	u	s	h	d	c	e
w	q	e	t	a	x	i	d	f

Getting from here to there

ACTIVITY 3

How do Ali, Ahmed, Salim, Sharifa, Shamsa and
Fatma get to school? Follow the lines and find out.

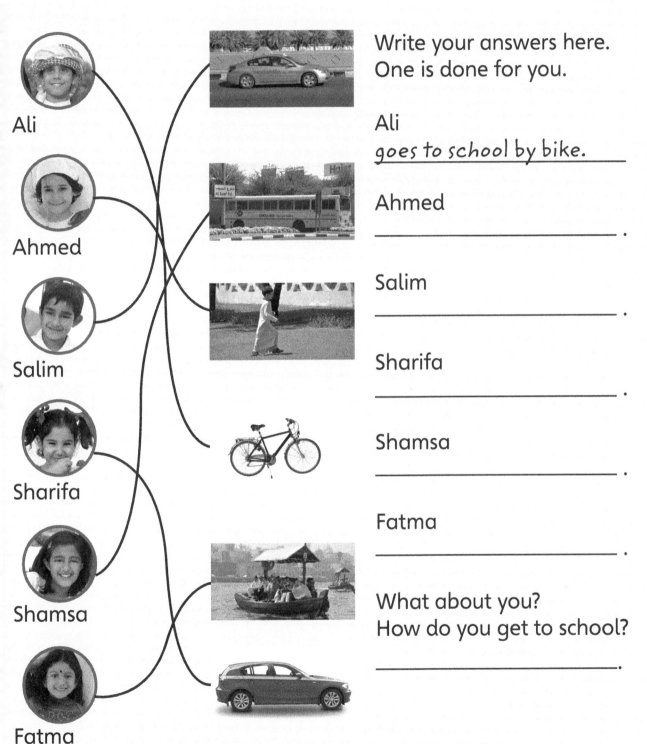

Ali

Ahmed

Salim

Sharifa

Shamsa

Fatma

Write your answers here.
One is done for you.

Ali
goes to school by bike. _____

Ahmed
_____.

Salim
_____.

Sharifa
_____.

Shamsa
_____.

Fatma
_____.

What about you?
How do you get to school?
_____.

8

Getting from here to there

Play this game with your friends.
Can you be the first to get to the beach?

100 **The beach**	99	98	97	96
81	82	83	84	85 Your cousin gives you a lift. Go to 92.
80	79	78	77	76
61 Stop at the shop to buy an ice-cream. Miss a go.	62	63	64	65
60	59	58 Your friend stops to give you a lift. Go to 65.	57	56
41	42	43	44	45
40 Stop at the bakery to buy a muffin. Miss a go.	39	38	37	36
21	22	23	24	25
20	19	18 Get a lift in a car. Go to 37.	17	16
1 **Start**	2	3	4	5 You find your bucket and spade. Go to the

9

95 lift in an abra. Go ght to the beach.	94	93	92	**91** Your bus breaks down. Miss a go.
86	87	88	89	90
75	74	73	72	71
66	67	68	69	70
55	54	**53** Stop at the toy shop to buy a ball. Miss a go.	52	51
46	47	48	49	50
35	34	33	**32** Your bike has a puncture. Miss a go.	31
26 u find a shortcut. Go to 34.	27	28	29	30
15	14	13	12	11
6	7	8	9	10

10

Colours everywhere

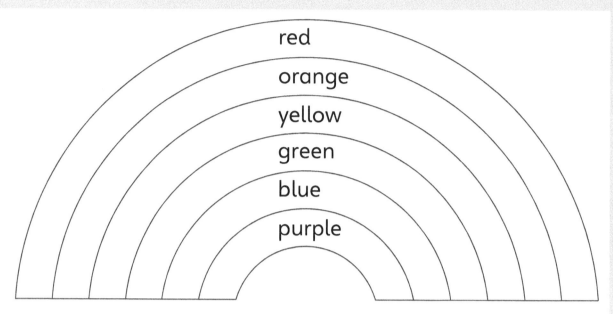

red

orange

yellow

green

blue

purple

Colour the rainbow.

The colours of the rainbow are red,　　　, green, orange, purple and blue.

II

Colours everywhere

Are these sentences true?

The first one is done for you.

This car is red.

No it isn't. It's blue.

These shoes are green.

_____

This door is yellow.

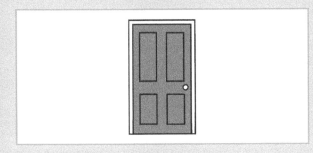

_____

This dress is black.

_____

This apple is blue.

_____

This banana is yellow.

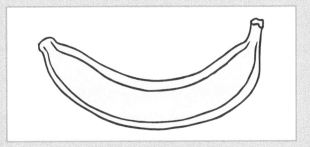

_____

Colours everywhere

Red and yellow make orange.

What do these colours make?
Colour the empty circle with the answer.

Blue and yellow.

Red and white.

Blue and red.

Mix them together and find out.

Use coloured pencils to write sentences like this:

Red and yellow make orange.

_____

_____

_____

13

Colours everywhere

Colour these objects.

Listen to your teacher.

Cover the pictures your teacher calls out. When you have covered all your pictures call out 'Pink Bananas!'

Colours everywhere

Count the balloons.

Complete the sentence.

I can see _____ red balloons, _____ yellow balloons, _____ light blue balloons, _____ dark blue balloons, _____ green balloons, _____ white balloons, _____ pink balloons and _____ purple balloons.

15

I can do many things!

Complete each sentence with the correct word.

I can _____ .

I can _____ .

I can _____ .

I can _____ .

I can _____ .

I can _____ .

16

I can do many things!

Tick the correct answer. The first one is done for you.

1 Can a baby drive?

Yes she can. ✗ No she can't. ✓

2 Can a fish sing?

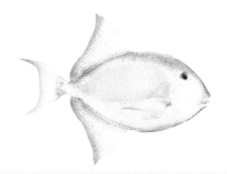

Yes it can.   No it can't.

3 Can a baker make cakes?

Yes he can.   No he can't.

4 Can a camel ski?

Yes it can.   No it can't.

5 Can a taxi driver drive?

Yes he can.   No he can't.

6 Can a banana dance?

Yes it can.   No it can't.

I can do many things!

Take turns to read the words.

Cross them out if you read them correctly.

jump	run	dance	eat	slide
hop	climb	sing	drink	run
eat	dance	slide	swing	climb
run	hop	eat	drink	jump
hop	slide	run	swing	jump

I can do many things!

The words in these sentences are mixed up.
Put them in the right order.

The first one is done for you.

1 can slide He.

He can slide.

2 swim He can.

_____

3 sing She can.

_____

4 He jump can.

_____

5 can run I.

_____

6 eat can I.

_____

Things I do every day

Sing this song with your teacher and do
the actions.

Here we go round the date palm tree, the date palm tree.

Here we go round the date palm tree

On a bright and sunny morning.

This is the way we brush our teeth, brush our teeth.

This is the way we brush our teeth

On a bright and sunny morning.

This is the way we wash our face, wash our face.

This is the way we wash our face

On a bright and sunny morning.

This is the way we brush our hair, brush our hair.

This is the way we brush our hair

On a bright and sunny morning.

This is the way we eat our breakfast, eat our breakfast.

This is the way we eat our breakfast

On a bright and sunny morning.

Here we go round the date palm tree, the date palm tree.

Here we go round the date palm tree

On a bright and sunny morning.

Things I do every day

Listen.
Write the correct letters for
the ends of the words.

I wa__ my face.

I bru__ my teeth.

I ge_ dresse_.

I pu_ on my shoes.

I ea_ breakfast.

I g_ to school.

Things I do every day

Write the sentences in the correct order.
The first one is done for you.

brush teeth

go to school

eat breakfast

put on my shoes

get dressed

wash my face

1 _I wash my face._ _____

2 _____

3 _____

4 _____

5 _____

6 _____

Things I do every day

Look at this breakfast.
Which foods can you see?

Label the food. One is done for you.

orange
juice

egg

apples

bread

cereal

grapes

cheese

What do you like to eat
for breakfast every day?

Draw a picture of the
things you like to eat.

23

Teaching notes

Introduction

The following notes provide suggestions for maximising learning opportunities when using Activity Book Level I of the *My Gulf world and me* series. The book is designed to provide multi-sensory and varied activities to encourage children to practise the target language in enjoyable ways. It is important to remember that young children learn through doing. They are much more likely to remember what they are taught if the lesson is fun. It is also important to remember that all children learn at different rates and in different ways. For example, some children may need extra help to complete the reading and writing activities. This will be the case if they have not yet been taught English phonemes and letter-to-sound associations.

A sense of success for all children should be incorporated into the lesson to develop the self-confidence of each child. Good self-esteem and confidence are essential to learning. A child who lacks self-confidence will be reluctant to practise a new language in case they fail.

All learners of a second language need to hear and practise the target language several times before they will remember it. So include as many opportunities as possible to do this through games and songs.

Shapes all around us

Activity I
Encourage the children to name items in the picture. Let them have fun searching for the shapes in the picture. Model the sentence for them to copy, for example 'I can see __ circles'. Children may be confused by the fact that 'c' is pronounced as an 's' in 'circle', so it is a good idea to explain that this sometimes happens in English when a 'c' is in front of an 'e' or 'i'.

Activity 2
Some children may not understand the concept of a shape having sides, so demonstrate this first by counting the sides of a square.

Activity 3
If possible, take the children to the souk to see geometric patterns in fabric and rugs or, if this isn't possible, bring some rugs into the classroom.

Activity 4
Give the children crayons or coloured pencils of the primary colours. Remind them that they can choose from any of the colours shown; not all circles need to be yellow, for example. When they have completed this, give them counters, such as a red diamond, to play shape bingo. Play this as a class first. Once the children are confident with both the shapes and the colours, they can play this game in pairs or small groups, taking turns to be the caller.

Activity 5
Sound out the individual letters in the word 'diamond'. Make sure that you use the phonemes and not the letter names, so 'd' is pronounced as in 'dish', not as 'dee'.

Getting from here to there

Activity 1
Encourage the children to name the forms of transport. Practise the phrase 'I can see four buses' and similar examples with the whole class.

Activity 2
Say each word (plane, bus, taxi, bike, abra, walk) slowly, emphasising the initial sound. Repeat several times if necessary. It is very common for young children to have difficulty in hearing the difference between 'b' and 'p'. They also often confuse 'b', 'd' and 'p' when reading and writing them. Even native speaker English children have difficulty with this.

Activity 3
After the children have finished the activity, encourage them to practise the target language in question-and-answer activities, for example 'How does Ali get to school? He goes by bike'.

Activity 4
Prepare the children for this game by introducing the rules and the extension vocabulary: 'get a lift', 'puncture', 'miss a go', 'breaks down', 'forget bucket and spade'.

Colours everywhere

Activity 1
Before the children complete the activity, recap on the names of the following colours using flashcards: red, yellow, green, orange, purple, blue. Choose six children to each hold a flashcard with a colour (face down). When they hear the name of their colour, they hold it up. If they line up in front of the class, this creates a rainbow effect.

Activity 2
As a class activity, read the sentences to the children. Elicit their responses, for example 'No it isn't. It's blue.' or 'Yes it is.' In pairs, the children could also put the questions to each other. This is a good opportunity to introduce contractions. Explain that when we speak, 'is not' becomes 'isn't'. Show the children how to write this.

Activity 3
Provide the children with a set of paints of the primary colours – red, yellow, blue, black and white. Encourage them to use the names of the colours as they experiment with mixing them. After they have done this, they can write sentences like the example, using coloured pencils.

Activity 4
Make sure that the children understand the following words – 'fish', 'dress', 'car', 'tree', 'apple', 'banana', 'door', 'horse', 'flower' and 'balloon' – by showing them these items on the flashcards. Provide them with coloured pencils and tell them that they can colour in the objects in any colours they choose. Play the game 'Pink Bananas'. Give each of the children a set of counters. Call out the names of the objects in different colours, for example 'a blue car'. If the child has a blue car, he/she covers it. The first child to cover all the objects on his/her board shouts out 'Pink Bananas!' and is the winner.

Activity 5
Introduce the vocabulary of light blue and dark blue. Count all the red balloons as a class activity to practise counting. The children then count the other balloons and write in the correct number.

I can do many things

Activity 1
Look at the pictures with the children and check that they know the language needed to describe the activities. Some children may need extra support to complete the writing activity so write the verbs 'sing', 'jump', 'eat', 'swim', 'run' and 'slide' on the board. Explain that these types of word are called verbs.

Activity 2
Read the sentences with the children. They are designed to be humorous so allow the children to joke about them. Children remember lessons when they have had fun. Elicit whole-class answers and encourage them to make up their own questions. The children then read the sentences independently if they are able, or with support if they need it, and select the correct answers. Remind them of contractions, for example that when we say 'cannot' it is normally spoken as 'can't'. Show them how this is written.

Activity 3
Write the verbs 'run', 'dance', 'sing', 'hop', 'slide', 'drink', 'jump', 'eat' and 'climb', on the board. As you write each individual letter, encourage the children to sound the words out. Point out that the 'b' at the end of 'climb' is silent. Choose individual children to come to the front of the class and mime the action of the verb as you write. When you are confident that all the children can recognise the words, arrange them in pairs or small groups and give each child a different-coloured pen. The children take turns to read a word. If they read it correctly, they cross it off. The first child to get a line of four words, either horizontally, vertically or diagonally, is the winner.

Activity 4
Stick paper with the following words on the board: 'slide', 'She' and 'can'. Ask a child to rearrange them into a sentence – 'She can slide'. The children rearrange the sentences in the activity in the same way.

Things I do every day

Activity 1
Sing the song with the children and mime the actions. If possible, play this in a circle in the playground. Don't expect them to be able to read every word of the song. However, if you read it with them and they follow the text with their finger it will help to familiarise them with new words.

Activity 2
Write the following phonemes on the board 'sh', 't', 'o' and 'd'. Sound them out and get the children to practise saying them. Read the sentences to the children and, as you do so, ask them to complete the verb endings in their activity books. Some children, especially those with auditory discrimination weaknesses, may find this difficult and need extra support.

Activity 3
Look at the pictures with the children and talk about which order they do the actions in. You could introduce the words 'first' and 'then' to talk about the sequence of actions. The children then write sentences to put the actions in the correct sequence. As an extension activity for more able children, you could introduce the time, for example 'I wake up at six o'clock.'

Activity 4
Using the flashcards, name and talk about the kinds of food people eat for breakfast. Talk about how people from different places like to eat different things at breakfast. Use magazines to find pictures of different types of food. The children can cut the pictures out and you can create a class collage of a buffet breakfast. Familiarise the children with the words 'orange juice', 'cereal', 'eggs', 'bread', 'cheese', 'grapes' and 'apples' before they complete the activity.

يمكنني فعل أشياء عديدة

النشاط ١

انظر إلى الصور مع الأطفال وتأكد من معرفتهم اللغة الضرورية لوصف الأنشطة. ارجع إلى البطاقات التعليمية؛ فقد يحتاج بعض الأطفال إلى مزيد من المساعدة لإكمال نشاط الكتابة، لذا اكتب الأفعال يغني (sing)، ويقفز (jump)، ويأكل (eat)، و يسبح (swim)، و يجري (run)، و ينزلق (slide) على اللوحة. واشرح أن هذا النوع من الكلمات يُسمى بالأفعال.

النشاط ٢

اقرأ العبارات مع الأطفال. فقد صممت لكي تتمتع بروح الدعابة، ولذلك دعهم يضحكون منها. فالأطفال يتذكرون الدروس إذا كانوا يمرحون فيها. احصل على إجابات الفصل بالكامل، وشجِّع الأطفال على طرح أسئلتهم الخاصة بهم. ثم يقرأ الأطفال العبارات بمفردهم، إذا استطاعوا ذلك، أو بمساعدة إذا احتاجوا إليها، ويختارون الإجابات الصحيحة. وذكّرهم بالاختصارات، على سبيل المثال، عندما يقولون "cannot" من الطبيعي أن تُنطق "can't". وضّح لهم كيفية كتابة ذلك.

النشاط ٣

اكتب الأفعال يجري (run)، ويرقص (dance)، ويغني (sing)، ويحجل (hop)، وينزلق (slide)، ويشرب (drink)، ويقفز (jump)، ويأكل (eat)، ويتسلق (climb) على اللوحة. وفي أثناء كتابة كل حرف على حدة، شجِّع الأطفال على نطق الكلمات بصوت مرتفع. ووضّح أن الحرف "b" في نهاية الكلمة "climb" لا يُنطق. اختر كل طفل على حدة للقدوم أمام الفصل وتقليد نطق الفعل وأنت تكتبه. عندما تكون على يقين من أن باستطاعة جميع الأطفال معرفة الكلمات، رتبهم في أزواج أو مجموعات صغيرة، وأعط كل طفل قلمًا ملونًا مختلفًا. ويتناوب الأطفال الأدوار لنطق أي كلمة. وفي حالة نطقهم لها بشكل صحيح، فإنهم يشطبونها. ويكون أول طفل يشطب سطرًا من أربع كلمات أفقياً أو عمودياً أو قطرياً هو الفائز.

النشاط ٤

الصق ورقة بها الكلمات التالية على اللوحة: التزلق يمكنها (slide She can). اطلب من أحد الأطفال إعادة ترتيب الكلمات في جملة مفيدة - يمكنها التزلق (She can slide). ويرتب الأطفال العبارات بالطريقة نفسها في النشاط.

أشياء أفعلها كل يوم

النشاط ١

غنِّ الأغنية مع الأطفال وقلد الأفعال. وإذا أمكن، غنِّ الأغنية مع اللعب في حلقة في الفناء. لا تتوقع منهم القدرة على قراءة كل كلمة في الأغنية. ومع هذا فإنك إذا قرأتها معهم وهم يتابعون النص بالمرور عليه بأصابعهم، فإن ذلك سيساعدهم على اعتياد الكلمات الجديدة.

النشاط ٢

اكتب المقاطع الصوتية التالية على اللوحة "sh" و"t" و"o" و"d". انطقها واجعل الأطفال يتدربون على نطقها. اقرأ العبارات على الأطفال، وفي أثناء قيامك بذلك، اطلب منهم إكمال نهايات الأفعال في كتب الأنشطة الخاصة بهم. قد يجد بعض الأطفال، خاصة من يعانون من ضعف في التمييز السمعي، هذا الأمر صعبًا ويحتاجون إلى مزيد من المساعدة.

النشاط ٣

انظر إلى الصور مع الأطفال، وتحدث عن الترتيب الذي يقومون فيه بالأفعال. ويمكنك إدخال الكلمتين "أولاً" (first) و"ثم" (and then) للحديث عن تسلسل الأفعال. ثم يكتب الأطفال العبارات لوضع الأفعال في التسلسل الصحيح. وكنشاط إضافي للأطفال الذين يتمتعون بقدرة أكبر، يمكنك إدخال الوقت. على سبيل المثال، "أستيقظ الساعة السادسة" (I wake up at six o'clock).

النشاط ٤

باستخدام البطاقات التعليمية، قم بتسمية أنواع الطعام التي يأكلها الأشخاص على الإفطار وتحدث عنها. وتحدث عن حب الأشخاص من أماكن مختلفة تناول أشياء مختلفة على الإفطار. واستخدم المجلات للبحث عن صور لأنواع الطعام المختلفة. يمكن للأطفال قص الصور، ويمكنك عمل لوحة فصل لبوفيه الإفطار. عوِّد الأطفال على الكلمات عصير برتقال (orange juice)، وحبوب (cereal)، وبيض (eggs)، وخبز (bread)، وجبن (cheese)، وعنب (grapes)، وتفاح (apples) قبل أن يُكملوا النشاط في كتاب الأنشطة الخاص بهم.

الألوان في كل مكان

النشاط ١

قبل أن يُنهي الأطفال النشاط، لخص أسماء الألوان التالية باستخدام البطاقات التعليمية: أحمر، أصفر، وردي، أخضر، برتقالي، أرجواني، أزرق. اختر سبعة أطفال لكي يمسك كل طفل منهم بطاقة تعليمية بها لون (اجعل وجهها لأسفل). وعندما يسمعون اسم اللون الموجود معهم، يرفعون البطاقة لأعلى. وعند اصطفافهم أمام الفصل، فإن هذا يخلق ظاهرة قوس قزح.

النشاط ٢

كنشاط مدرسي، اقرأ العبارات على الأطفال. واحصل على إجاباتهم، على سبيل المثال، "لا، ليست كذلك. إنها زرقاء" (.No it isn't. It's blue) أو "نعم إنها كذلك" (Yes it is) كما يستطيع كل طفلين طرح الأسئلة على بعضهما. إنها فرصة جيدة لتعريفهم الاختصارات.
اشرح كيف أننا عندما ننطق "is not" تصبح "isn't". ووضح لهم كيفية كتابة ذلك.

النشاط ٣

وفر لهم مجموعة من أقلام الألوان الأساسية – الأحمر، والأصفر، والأزرق، والأسود، والأبيض. وشجِّعهم على استخدام أسماء الألوان وهم يتدربون على مزجها. بعد قيامهم بذلك، يمكنهم كتابة جمل كالمثال باستخدام أقلام رصاص ملونة.

النشاط ٤

تأكد من أن الأطفال يفهمون الكلمات التالية - سمكة (fish)، وفستان (dress)، وسيارة (car)، وشجرة (tree)، وتفاحة (apple)، وموز (banana)، وباب (door)، وحصان (horse)، وزهرة (flower)، وبالونه (balloon) – من خلال توضيح العناصر الموجودة على البطاقات التعليمية. وفر لهم أقلام رصاص ملونة، وأخبرهم أن بإمكانهم تلوين الأشياء بالألوان التي يختارونها. مَارس لعبة الموز الوردي (Pink Bananas). أعط كل طفل من الأطفال مجموعة من القطع. انطق بصوت مرتفع أسماء الأشياء بألوان مختلفة، مثل سيارة زرقاء. وإذا كان مع الطفل أو الطفلة سيارة زرقاء، يقوم أو تقوم بتغطيتها. وأول طفل يغطي جميع الأشياء الموجودة في لوحته يصيح قائلًا "!Pink Bananas"، ويكون هو الفائز.

النشاط ٥

أدخل مفردات الأزرق الفاتح والأزرق الداكن. وقم بعد البالونات الحمراء كنشاط مدرسي لممارسة العد. ثم يقوم الأطفال بعد البالونات الأخرى وكتابة الرقم الصحيح.

الانتقال من هنا إلى هناك

النشاط ١

شجِّع الأطفال على تسمية وسائل المواصلات. وعليك بالتدرب على العبارات "يمكنني رؤية أربع حافلات" (I can see four buses) وما إلى ذلك مع الفصل كله.

النشاط ٢

انطق كل كلمة (طائرة (plane)، وحافلة (bus)، وسيارة أجرة (taxi)، ودراجة (bike)، وعبّارة (abra)، السير على الأقدام (walk)) ببطء مع التركيز على طريقة نطق أول حرف. أعد ذلك عدة مرات، إذا احتاج الأمر. فمن الشائع جدًا أن يجد الأطفال الصغار صعوبة في التمييز بين الحرفين "b" و"p". كما أنهم غالبًا ما يشعرون بالحيرة عند قراءة الأحرف "b"، و"d"، و"p" وكتابتها. حتى الأطفال الناطقين باللغة الإنجليزية يواجهون صعوبة في ذلك.

النشاط ٣

بعد أن ينتهي الأطفال من النشاط، شجِّعهم على ممارسة أنشطة السؤال والجواب باللغة المستهدفة مثل "كيف يذهب علي إلى المدرسة؟" (?How does Ali get to school) "يذهب بالدراجة" (He goes by bike).

النشاط ٤

قم بتهيئة الأطفال لهذه اللعبة عن طريق تعريفهم بالقواعد والمفردات الزائدة في الكلمات: احصل على توصيلة (get a lift)، ثقب (puncture)، ضربة فاشلة (miss a go)، يتعطل (breaks down).

المقدمة

توفر الملاحظات التالية اقتراحات للوصول إلى أقصى مدى من فرص التعلم عند استخدام المستوى ١ من كتاب الأنشطة من سلسلة My Gulf World and Me series. وقد تم تصميم هذا الكتاب لتوفير سبل متعددة الحواس المستهدفة لتشجيع الأطفال على ممارسة اللغة المستهدفة بطرق ممتعة. ومن المهم أن نتذكر أن الأطفال الصغار يتعلمون من خلال الممارسة العملية. ومن الجائز جدًا أن يتذكروا ما يتعلمونه، إذا كان الدرس ممتعًا. كما أنه من المهم أن نتذكر أن كل الأطفال يتعلمون بمعدلات مختلفة وبطرق مختلفة. فعلى سبيل المثال، قد يحتاج بعض الأطفال إلى مساعدة إضافية لاستكمال أنشطة القراءة والكتابة. وسيكون هذا هو الحال إذا لم يكونوا قد عُلِّموا طريقة نطق الكلمات في اللغة الإنجليزية وارتباط الحرف بالصوت.

يجب أن يتضمن الدرس الإحساس بالنجاح لدى جميع الأطفال لتعزيز ثقة كل طفل بنفسه. ويُعد الاعتزاز الجيد بالنفس والثقة ضرورة للتعلم. فالطفل الذي تنقصه الثقة بالنفس سيصبح مترددًا في ممارسة اللغة الجديدة في حال فشله.

ويحتاج جميع المتعلمين للغة ثانية إلى سماع اللغة المستهدفة وممارستها عدة مرات قبل أن يحفظوها. ولذلك، قم بإتاحة أكبر عدد ممكن من الفرص لأداء ذلك من خلال الألعاب والأغاني.

الأشكال في كل مكان حولنا

النشاط ١

شجِّع الأطفال على تسمية الأشياء الموجودة بالصورة. ودعهم يستمتعون بالبحث عن الأشكال الموجودة في الصورة. هناك إجمالي X دائرة (circle)، وX مربع (square)، وX مستطيل (rectangle)، وX مثلث (triangle)، وX معين (diamond)، وX هلال (crescent)، وX نجمة (star) في الصورة. اكتب عبارة نموذجًا يحتذون به، مثل "يمكنني مشاهدة __ دائرة" (I can see __ circles). قد يصاب الأطفال بالحيرة من حقيقة أن الحرف "c" يُنطق مثل الحرف "s" في كلمة "circle"، لذا فإنها لفكرة جيدة أن تشرح أن هذا يحدث أحيانًا في اللغة الإنجليزية، عندما يسبق الحرف "c" الحرف "e" أو "i".

النشاط ٢

قد لا يستوعب بعض الأطفال مفهوم الشكل المضلع، لذا اشرح ذلك أولاً عن طريق عد أضلاع مربع.

النشاط ٣

إن أمكن، اصطحب الأطفال إلى السوق لمشاهدة الأشكال الهندسية على النسيج والسجاد، أو إذا لم يكن ذلك ممكنًا، احضر بعض السجاد إلى الفصل.

النشاط ٤

أعط الأطفال أقلام شمع أو أقلام رصاص ملونة بالألوان الأساسية. قل لهم إن بإمكانهم اختيار أحد الألوان الموضحة، ولا يوجد هناك داع أن تكون جميع الدوائر صفراء، على سبيل المثال. وعندما تنتهي من هذا الأمر، أعطهم مع القطع قطعًا مثل معين أحمر للعب لعبة تشكيل الأشكال بنجو. ومارس هذه اللعبة في الفصل أولاً. وبمجرد أن يصبح لدى الأطفال الثقة في الأشكال والألوان، يمكنهم ممارسة هذه اللعبة في أزواج أو مجموعات صغيرة، ويتناوبون القيام بدور المنادي.

النشاط ٥

انطق كل حرف من الحروف التي تحتوي عليها كلمة "معين" (diamond) على حدة. وتأكد من استخدام طريقة نطق الحروف لا طريقة أسماء الحروف، بحيث يُنطق الحرف "d" كما هو في كلمة "dish" وليس "dee".